God And Choice
And Life Or Death

God And Choice And Life Or Death

By

Ellen K. Gordon

This book is dedicated to my husband, and very best friend, James, who has loved me unconditionally for 42 years. I thank him for his valuable and unwavering love.

ARPress
45 Dan Road Suite 5
Canton MA 02021

Hotline:	1(888) 821-0229
Fax:	1(508) 545-7580

Ordering Information:
Quantity sales. Special discounts are available on quantity purchases by corporations, associations, and others. For details, contact the publisher at the address above.

Printed in the United States of America.

ISBN-13:	Paperback	979-8-89356-676-5
	eBook	979-8-89356-677-2

Library of Congress Control Number: 2024903604

Table Of Contents

Preface

I heard on the inside of me one day… "Do you think all of the authors of the bible were special? Do you think I made them any different than I made you or anyone else? I didn't. I didn't make any person any different, or better than anyone else. He or she simply inclined his or her ears unto me, with hearts desirous of hearing from me. Through his or her obedience, all listened to what I had to say and then wrote it down."

Later on that day I thought to myself, surely all of the authors of the bible were not already authors. It does not record anything they had prior written. I thought, certainly they had not experienced everything God gave them to record. Paul had not experienced anything for God through Christ, and yet wrote two-thirds of the New Testament. God called them holy. (Ref. 2 Pet. 1:21) They were not holy because He made them that way. They were holy because they chose obedience to His will.

Years ago while reading the bible, I thought, God sure did talk directly to the people back then, and they talked back to Him. It seemed like He initiated many of the conversations. I thought about that for many years before I knew how to ask Him if he would talk to me.

I later found out that God is not stingy with His Word. That He will talk to anyone that desires to hear from Him. However, He is not so desperate as to talk to someone that does not extend to Him their undivided attention, yet He desires to have a relationship with everyone. Now I can say He and I talk regularly. I always write it down.

God and Choice and Life or Death have been a part of me for as long as I can remember. I started reading the bible on my own when I was fourteen years old. I didn't understand it then, but I felt led to read it. After which I would hide under my bed and talk to God. I was called names of course by one of my siblings. I can't remember a time when I was not trying to figure out the choices of life, and God, and writing it all down. Since becoming able to hear from Him, I often steal away to a quiet place that He and I might be alone.

With God, as the ultimate authority, or author, I believe this book will enlighten many, teach others, and spiritually nourish those who are underfed.

God's Word is important to me. I know that he loves me, and will lead me the right way. With all of me, I desire to hear from Him.

Introduction

God, and Choice, and Life, or Death, in that order, has danced around in my head for many years. I have since found it to be a profound truth. God is the basis of this truth. He is life and the giver of life. He has given mankind the choice of life, through Christ, which comes with responsibility. Once we recognize that this choice is a right to be responsible, it will cause us to walk uprightly before Him.

It is my personal belief that all of life has a creator. I have chosen to call Him, Him, and I have chosen to call Him God. I say this because I recognize beginnings, origins, traditions, etc., and know this is relatively normal considering my roots. However, I have made my deliberate choice.

I believe God's choice for mankind is for him to be blessed, or empowered to prosper. I believe God has already made all of the necessary provisions to live a prosperous life. Provisions that will cause people to love one another. Provisions that marriages can prosper, and last. Provisions that all of mankind can be fed, clothed, and kept. The provision to cause prosperity of the heart. Then we will forgive others, simply because we recognize we also needed to be forgiven. I believe the ability to conquer all of the ills in this world presently exists, because God has finished His creation, and there is no lack in it.

That provision is Christ. He is the fulfillment of all that we need on the earth. God gave dominion over the earth to the human being species that He created and made. We are responsible for the positive growth and continuance of this world. This cannot happen without recognition of God, and the set order. To many like-minded believers, this is Christianity. We choose Jesus and life. It is not a religion, occult, or any other entity formed by humankind that divides, and separates. Real Christianity unifies.

Following God through Christ is a commitment of heart to love God with your total being, and your neighbor as yourself. This is life through Christ, entire, complete, and wanting nothing.

The human being species was given a choice by God at creation. This choice cannot be debated by humankind. It is settled. In the book of Deuteronomy, Chapter 30, verses 19-20 KJV says,

" I call heaven and earth to record this day against you, that I have set before you, life and death, blessing and cursing: therefore choose life, that both thou and thy seed may live: that thou mayest love the Lord thy God, and that thou mayest obey His voice, and that thou mayest cleave unto Him, for He is thy life, and the length of thy days: that thou mayest dwell in the land which the Lord sware unto thy fathers, to Abraham, to Isaac, and to Jacob, to give them."

I, as well as many like-minded believers, recognize and acknowledge that we have this choice. We have committed our lives to God, through Jesus Christ. We purposefully and deliberately live by the covenant God made with Abraham, (and to us). (Gal. 3:8-9 KJV) This is a choice within us that we've activated by the spoken word of our mouths, given by God. Life! After making this choice, humankind can do nothing to hinder or stop it. It is established, complete, entire, and wanting nothing.

I define this choice as an established, intangible mechanism at the core of our being, which is activated by our will for our lives through the spoken word of our mouths. This choice is sometimes ignored, and or unrecognized, however, it is always present, and available to us. Its purpose is to keep us (our spirit) in the hands of freedom. A place within us where we are always safe, where we are sane, and where we recognize the greatness that is within us through Christ Jesus, our Lord. This is not the freedom of footloose, wild, and fancy-free, but the freedom of kings and priests. This freedom enables us our responsible rights. We understand that God is responsible and the only right, (Ref. Deut. 32:4), and only through Him can anyone obtain rights. No one has the right or (God) on his side to do anything unless it is through Him, which is the basis of truth.

In the book of John, Chapter 8, verses 31-32, KJV, Jesus said,

"If you continue in my word, then are ye my disciples indeed; and ye shall know the truth, and the truth shall make you free."

First He instructs us to continue. We cannot pick up the Word of God, and put it down, with yet still the expectation of receiving what it says. Our continuance in the Word is the key to our forthcoming knowledge and revelation. Jesus says, "Then are ye my disciples indeed." Disciples are disciplined ones that recognize the order of God, and will themselves to carry it out. These orders carried out, are the physical evidence of the disciplined spirits, willed from the soul (mind). This is the order of God. When your spirit (heart) is disciplined toward God, your soul wills your body to follow through.

To continue in the Word is to do the Word, and to do the deeds. And to do the deeds as Christ did them ensures life eternal. The book of John, Chapter 14, verses 12-14 KJV, says, "Verily, verily, I say unto you, He that believeth on me, the works that I do shall he do also; and greater works than these shall he do; because I go unto my Father. And whatsoever ye shall ask in my name, that will I do, that the Father may be glorified in the Son. If ye shall ask anything in my name, I will do it."

In making this choice we are the children of God. Romans, Chapter 8, verse 17 says, "...and if children, then heirs; heirs of God, and joint-heirs with Christ;

if so, be that we suffer with Him, that we may be also glorified together."

Know this day that you have the choice of God that supersedes all others.

The Beginning

"In the beginning, God created the heavens and the earth. The earth was formless and empty, and darkness covered the deep waters. And the Spirit of God was hovering over the surface of the waters. Then God said, "Let there be light," and there was light. Genesis 1:1-3NLT

God spoke the word, and by faith created heaven and the earth. As likewise, He spoke the light into existence from within himself. Verses four through twenty-five list several things that God created and then made completing the earth with water, land, sky, vegetation, livestock, flying fowl, fish, and separating the day from the darkness which He called night.

"Then God said, "Let us make human beings in our image, to be like us. They will reign over the fish in the sea, the birds in the sky, the livestock, all the wild animals on the earth, and the small animals that scurry along the ground. So God created human beings in His own image. In the image of God He created them; male and female He created them." Genesis 1:26-27 NLT

God's choice for mankind was for them to be like Him, and so they were. They were complete in every way. Mankind's totality was abundantly blessed. Their spirit, soul, and body, responded to God in every way. There is no lack in God, and there was no lack in human beings.

"Then the Lord God formed the man from the dust of the ground. He breathed the breath of life into the man's nostrils, and the man became a living person." Genesis 2:7NLT

When God formed this human being and breathed the breath of life into his nostrils, every human who has ever been born, and every human that will ever be born, was present at that time in that human. He breathed the breath of life into the human being species. Not Adam only, but human beings were introduced on the earth. We were all present long before we were born to our parents. (Ref. Jeremiah 1:5) Our spirit is who we are. The birth of the body was formed so that we could live on this three-dimensional earth.

"The Lord God placed the man in the Garden of Eden to tend and watch over it. But the Lord God warned him, "You may freely eat the fruit of every tree in the garden – except the tree of the knowledge of good and evil. If you eat its fruit, you are sure to die." Genesis 2:15-17 NLT

The tree of the knowledge of good and evil was the first sign of choice in the world. Everything that had been created, had to then be made and put on the earth. (Ref. Gen. 2:4-5) Being that God created mankind in His own image, humans were given a choice, free will, and dominance, before the foundation of the world. They were like God. God made humans and put them on the earth to represent Him. The tree of the knowledge of good and evil had a purpose, but it was not for food. That tree justified a difference from all the other trees, that a choice would be enforced upon the earth. It was the physical representation of a choice being implemented on the earth. Everything on the earth was first created (using the spoken word only) spiritually by God, then made (using something tangible) by God, and put onto the earth.

"Then the Lord God said, "It is not good for the man to be alone. I will make a helper who is just right for him." Genesis 2:18. NLT

The word alone means all-in-one. The spirit of the man and the woman were present, housed in one body, made from the dust of the ground. Not that the woman was not present. She, as well as all past, present, and future human beings were spirit beings in the one body since God created male and female back in Genesis 1:26. He made one body from the dust in Genesis 2:7 that produced the flesh of all humankind. (Ref. Acts 17:26)

"So the Lord God caused the man to fall into a deep sleep. While the man slept, the Lord God took out one of the man's ribs and closed up the opening. Then the Lord God made a woman from the rib, and he brought her to the man. "At last!" the man exclaimed. "This one is bone from my bone, and flesh from my flesh! She will be called 'woman,' because she was taken from 'man.'" Genesis 2:21-23 NLT The spirit that

3

represented the female species was present but needed a body to live on the earth.

"Now the serpent was more subtle than any beast of the field which the Lord God had made. And he said unto the woman, Yea, hath God said, Ye, shall not eat of every tree of the garden? And the woman said unto the serpent, We may eat of the fruit of the trees of the garden: But of the fruit of the tree which is in the midst of the garden, God hath said, Ye shall not eat of it, neither shall ye touch it, lest ye die. And the serpent said unto the woman, Ye shall not surely die:" Genesis 3:1-4 KJV

God didn't say "neither shall you touch it," the woman added that in.

"And when the woman saw that the tree was good for food and that it was pleasant to the eyes, and a tree to be desired to make one wise, she took of the fruit thereof, and did eat, and gave also unto her husband with her; and he did eat." Gen. 3:6 KJV

The problem came after they ate of the fruit, which God had said they should not eat, lest they die. And died they did from the glorious, whole, sound, powerful, and complete human beings they were. Their disobedience immediately separated them from the Father, and it became necessary for the human being to need a savior. One that would pave the way for humans to be able to come back to God, and be whole in every way. That one is Jesus.

"And they heard the voice of the Lord God walking in the garden in the cool of the day: and Adam and his wife hid from the presence of the Lord God amongst the trees of the garden. And the Lord God called unto Adam, and said unto him, where art thou? And he said, I heard thy voice in the garden, and I was afraid because I was naked, and I hid. And he said, Who told thee that thou was naked? Hast thou ate of the tree, whereof I commanded thee that thou shouldest not eat?" Genesis 3:8-11 KJV

Not only did he know he was naked but said that he was afraid. Fear is always there lurking after disobedience. Then, because he was naked, he hid. Shame is also present. Sin had entered the earth through the disobedient acts of the first man and woman. Disobedience, shame, and fear covered them, and they died just as God said. Their spirit was disconnected from the life source, therefore their physical being was susceptible to sin, sickness, and death.

After the fall of Adam, or separation from God, all of mankind is then born in sin. At birth, we are no longer the great beings God created and made in the beginning. Before mankind's fall, mankind would not have participated in fear, sickness, disease, shame, jealousy, or death. These all came out of sin. Therefore, we are all born in sin and need a savior. As children, we are closer to God and his ways than when we grow up. As we grow, we learn and are drawn by the sinful nature that is within us from birth to more sin-filled things. Many times people begin to feel like these sin-filled ways are normal because they have been with them since birth. But they are not what God intended for His creation.

Many people engage in sin-filled things and think that because they say they were born that way is permission for them to continue therein. We were all born in sin and shaped in iniquity according to Psalm 51:5. Yet we are all the children of our heavenly Father, and His desire is for all to be saved, or brought back to Him through the receiving of His only begotten Son, Jesus Christ, our Lord.

Sickness and disease do not come from God. Sin is in the world, and the farther away from God we allow ourselves to get, the closer to sin, sickness, and disease we get. God is life, health, and peace. Sin brings sickness, shame, disease, and death. It is necessary that we purposefully choose God, and life, which are synonymous, or we will choose Satan, sickness, and death by default.

"For God so loved the world that He gave His only begotten Son, that whosoever believeth in Him should not perish, but have everlasting life." John 3:16 KJV

God, having sent Jesus, we have an advocate.

1st John 2:1 KJV says, "My little children, these things write I unto you, that ye sin not. And if any man sin, we have an advocate with the Father, Jesus Christ the righteous..."

We have a way out. However, we must choose Him, and receive Him as our savior. Jesus came into a sinful world and remained sinless by obeying the Father and reversing the curse. Adam's disobedience was reversed by Jesus' obedience. (Ref. Rom. 5:19) Now through

Christ, those of us who have chosen Christ, is back with God, the Father, as it was in the beginning.

Proverbs 18:21 KJV reads, "Death and life are in the power of the tongue: and they that love it shall eat the fruit thereof."

Our words are powerful. Everything depends upon the choices we make, whether we will have life or death, go forward or backward, increase or decrease, have or have not.

"And on the seventh day God ended His work which He had made, and he rested on the seventh day from all His work which he had made." Genesis 2:2 KJV

God's creation was finished. The plan or way for mankind to continue on the earth in life, although he had sinned, was given through Jesus. Jesus existed at the beginning with God. The physical way made for Him to come to the earth, and save the world was made through the womb of a virgin girl. He walked the earth carrying out the order of God. When His purpose here was complete, John records Jesus saying on the cross:

"It is finished" 'and he bowed his head, and gave up the ghost.' John 19:30 KJV

His work is done. Forgiveness has been given. And life as God intended receive Christ Jesus.

"It Could Happen To Anyone."

This is one of the most untrue statements that float about in society today. Every time something happens that is serious, which is every day somewhere, you can look forward to hearing someone say, "It could happen to anyone." The statement suggests that we have no control over our lives. It's as though we make no choices or decisions about the things in which we take part.

Everything that happens is a result of something else, whether it is good or bad. People make choices every day that brings results, many times without recognition or thought about the results. Because a person did not choose to consider the result of his action, does not mean it could happen to anyone. It only means it could happen to that one.

The book of Haggai, Chapter 1:6-7 records this interesting view; "Ye have sown much, and bring in little; ye eat, but ye have not enough; ye drink, but ye are not filled with drink; ye clothe you, but there is none warm, and he that earneth wages to put it into a bag with holes. Thus saith the Lord of the host; consider your ways."

The prophet Haggai goes even further. He said, even though you eat, and drink, you are not filled. But that you should consider your ways, meaning your motives. Our motives have more to do with a situation, and its outcome than we sometimes realize. What is the motive behind the action you just took? According to Haggai, what is going on, on the inside of us plays an even greater part in the results.

We should always be conscious of our choices, and aware of the results. We decide our life's happenings. Every seed that I plant into my life, I should expect to get exactly what that seed produces. Things don't just happen, they are always the result of a prior action, whether recognized or not.

Those of us who have purposefully chosen God through Christ, and life, have realized this choice that has been given. How so very often people leave to chance their lives to contend with. Chance is not on your side when it comes to this life. We must choose God, through Jesus Christ, or get God's enemy by default.

To not recognize our power of choice is at its least detrimental, and many times fatal. This choice was given by God, before the foundation of the world. Those that don't realize they have a choice in life, as well as a choice of life, are they that are fighting others for it. By not recognizing our power of choice, we forfeit our God-given right. A choice is something that was made available to each one of us in the beginning, and it is activated by the spoken word of our mouths.

Recognizing the choices we make, and being aware of the results disallows the thinking, "it could happen to anyone." The consciousness of one's decision increases the expectation of receiving exactly what was desired. With your new perspective, and your power of choice, you will begin to notice that things don't just happen, but you make choices expecting the desired result.

It has been said, "We are the choices that we have made." To allow this to be so, would cause us to be responsible for ourselves, and our errors. Some are not prepared to accept this truth. It is sometimes easier to place blame elsewhere.

Once again, this is a choice that we all have, only we don't all know that it exists. This is the power of God, and His availability of protective custody to whosoever will. Under His umbrella, there is life, health, and freedom. Outside of His umbrella, there are all kinds of bondage, disease, and unnecessary death. You can choose God and life, or you cannot choose and have chosen by default. After default, you can just accept all the bondage and believe, "it could happen to anyone."

Ephesians, Chapter 3, verse 19 say: "And to know the love of Christ, which passeth knowledge that ye might be filled with all the fullness of God." The apostle, Paul says to know the love of Christ, passeth knowledge, and because of knowing that love, we will be filled with all the fullness of God. Either we do not believe that, or we do not understand what that means for us. Those of us that know the love of Christ, have within us more than learned knowledge and are therefore capable of accomplishing great things because we are filled with all the fullness of God.

This is a wonderful thing God has done for those that have chosen Him, and no one can change it. God's ways are higher than the ways of the world. In choosing Him, and submitting ourselves unto His ways, we too become higher than the ways of the world. Worldly issues cannot ultimately affect us, because they cannot affect God. We (our spirit) are with Him now. Not after we die, and go to heaven, but now. We are not ultimately limited by this temporary house called a body we are in. We are spirit beings, with great capabilities.

The apostle, Paul continues in Ephesians, Chapter 3, verse 20, by saying, "Now unto him, that is able to do exceeding abundantly above all that we ask or think, according to the power that worketh in us..." God is able and willing to do great things in us. However, it is according to the power of God that the believer allows working through him. God does not force His ways upon any one. The amount of God's power that works in a believer's life is up to that believer, not God. He has already chosen us, by giving Jesus, that we may have life; now we have to choose Him, by allowing Him to live and work through us.

Joshua, Chapter 24, verse 15 records, "And if it seems evil unto you to serve the Lord, choose you this day whom ye will serve; whether the gods which your fathers served that were on the other side of the flood or the gods of the Amorites, in whose land ye dwell: but as for me and my house, we will serve the Lord."

Every happening is initiated by something or someone. Receiving and activating our power of choice which was given by God brings life. Life with God through Christ is more than just breathing, it is abundant! Things don't just happen. You can choose life through Christ, or you can choose not to choose, and get Satan by default.

Unrecognized Choices

Proverbs 14: 12 says, "There is a way that seemeth right unto a man, but the end thereof are the ways of death."

That way is through the deceitfulness of Satan. Everything about him is deceitful and leads to death. He is the father of lies. (John 8:44) Devastation and destruction is his pleasure. Secrets and seclusion is his domain. Hidden areas, undercover, and darkness is his playing field. He is cunning and crafty; subtle and clever. He is a thief, and pretense is his friend. He walks about as a roaring lion seeking whom he may devour. (Ref.1Peter 5:8) He is an evil spirit, yet ineffective alone. Only through the allowed expression of a human being does he become empowered and able to cause harm. Some of his traits are selfishness, deceitfulness, envious, jealousy, hateful, and unthankful. He's a liar. Who will allow him to use their heart, their hands, or their mouth?

1st John 5:11-12, records, "And this is the record, that God hath given to us eternal life, and this life is

His Son. He that hath the Son, hath life; and he that hath not the Son of God hath not life."

This life is through Christ Jesus, our Lord. He is life and light. He is love and strength, and in Him, you can put your trust. "Cast your cares upon Him, for He cares for you." (1 Peter 5:7) He can do exceeding abundantly above all that we ask or think according to the power that worketh in us. (Ephesians 3:20) He is the author and finisher of our faith (Ref. Hebrews 12:1) therefore, we believe to receive all provisions necessary to live this life well. He has made available to every born again believer the Holy Spirit. The fruits of the Holy Spirit are love, joy, peace, longsuffering, gentleness, goodness, faith, meekness, and temperance. (Ref. Gal. 5:22-23)

This Spirit is only effective through the allowed expression of a human being. God gave the Holy Spirit to come and live inside of the human being. After we are born again, the Holy Spirit can take up residence inside of us. Who will invite him into their heart? Who will allow themselves to be used by the Spirit of God? Who will invite Him in, to take up residence in their heart, that He may use their mouth or their hands for His service?

Human beings make choices every day, all day, not recognizing many of them. We chose the spirit that is presently operating in our bodies. Many have chosen the evil one. Some by deliberate choice, and some by default, by not choosing Christ. Whether you believe it or not, the inner man of every human being has a lord. You may not have chosen the Lord, God, but you still have a lord. And he is influencing your heart and thinking about the junk ways of this world. Proverbs, Chapter 23, verse 7 KJV say,

"For as he (a man) thinketh in his heart, so is he:" Choose the Lord, God, for He is good, or that other fellow who is described as walking about as a roaring lion seeking whom he may devour. Seeking those who are empty of the light of Christ. Seeking those who are not sober, not vigilant, as it says in 1 Peter 5 that he may pounce at his will. The choice is yours.

The ability to make choices in life is the floor of the mind. Everything else is built upon it. The mind is the main component of the soul, also housing the will, the emotions, the imagination, and the intellect.

Our soul is the link that connects our spirit to our body. Our spirit is greater than our body. Without our soul, which allows our body choice or free will, our spirit would overtake our body. That is what is commonly known as physical death. Death occurs when the soul or mind shuts down or surrenders all, and the spirit being greater takes precedence over the body. This is how human beings can remain alive through trying times by choosing life by the strength and renewing of our minds to the Word of God. It maintains a balance between the spirit and the body. However, many times unrecognized, this choice of life or death is made in the soul.

The bible instructs us to renew our mind, which means to make it new by casting out bad or evil thoughts, and all cares and worrisome thoughts that are contrary to the Word of God. "Casting down imaginations, and every high thing that exalts itself against the knowledge of God, and bringing into captivity every thought to the obedience of Christ;" 2 Cor. 10: 5 KJV

'Isaiah 26:3 KJV says, "Thou wilt keep him in perfect peace, whose mind is stayed on thee: because he trusteth in thee."

It is of the utmost importance to renew our minds often, as the bible instructs. There is much in the world to influence the mind away from God. If you allow your mind to weaken by watching too much television, and countless other things, you could find yourself in a world of trouble. You would begin to think about the foolishness that's often on television and think it could happen to you. The day that Satan gets you to believe that lie he starts moving in for the kill.

"The thief cometh not, but for to steal, and to kill, and to destroy: I am come that they might have life and that they might have it more abundantly." (John 10:10) Jesus is letting it be known what the purpose of the enemy is, and what His purpose is for us. Abundant life for all who believe.

A mind that is not nourished with the Word of God is heading for devastation, destruction, and or death.

Being more conscious of the choices we make daily would help our lives to be more meaningful. The power of choice is a great thing God has given us. He has fulfilled us in every way. He is our life.

"I call heaven and earth to record this day against you, that I have set before you, life and death, blessing and cursing: therefore choose life, that both thou and thy seed may live: That thou mayest love the Lord thy God, and that thou mayest obey His voice, and that thou mayest cleave unto Him: for He is thy life, and the length of thy days: that thou mayest dwell in the land which the Lord sware unto thy fathers, to Abraham, to Isaac, and to Jacob, to give them." Deut. 30:19-20

Through Christ Jesus, life is given. We can have it if we choose.

Perfect Obedience

Jesus chose obedience to His Father's will to come to the earth in the flesh. He never allowed His mind to think on His flesh as being who He was. He knew that He was a spirit and that His body added nothing to Him. He was complete without it.

We too are spirits, and when we see ourselves this way, without thought of our bodies as being who we are, we come closer to being the empowered beings God intended. When we give our minds (soul) over to thinking on our flesh, it limits our ability to activate the power of God into our lives. The more attention we pay to our bodies, which is the least of who we are, the further away from God we get.

In John, Chapter 4, verse 24 NLT Jesus says,

"For God is a Spirit, so those who who worship Him must worship in spirit and in truth."

Spirit and truth are the same things. Whatever is of the Spirit, is the truth, and whatever is the truth is of the Spirit. (Ref. 1 John 5:6) This is not the human being's spirit, but the Spirit of God.

Matthew, Chapter 4, verses 1-4 KJV says," Then was Jesus led up of the Spirit into the wilderness to be tempted of the devil. And when He had fasted forty days and forty nights, He was afterward an hungred. And when the tempter came to Him, he said, if thou be the Son of God, command that these stones be made bread. But He answered and said, It is written, Man shall not live by bread alone, but by every word that proceedeth out of the mouth of God."

Jesus was greater than His hunger because He was greater than His body.

The spirit can live without the body, and it does before the body, as well as after it leaves the body. (Ref. Jeremiah 1:4-5) The body cannot live without the spirit, regardless of how much nourishment, exercise, or eating an apple a day. (Ref. James 2:26) After the soul (mind) surrenders, and the spirit takes over, that's it for the body.

In John, Chapter 8, verse 52, the Jews were talking with Jesus about Abraham and the prophets being dead, and Jesus was saying they are not dead because the spirit lives forever. They did not know anything about the spirit. They were law-abiding, which means they governed their bodies according to the laws of Moses, which caused them to think, and operate from the "outside." Jesus works from the "inside," of the human being where the Holy Spirit resides. Our spirit is the real person.

Further into this chapter, verses 56-58, Jesus says, "Your father Abraham rejoiced to see my day: and he

19

saw it, and was glad." Then said the Jews unto Him, "Thou art not yet fifty years old, and hast thou seen Abraham?" Jesus said unto them, "Verily, verily, I say unto you, Before Abraham was, I am."

Jesus was telling them that He was present even before Abraham. He had not yet been born on the earth, but He existed long before then. He didn't say "I was," he said, "I am," which means continuous. He has never stopped being. Because he was presently in a body, didn't mean he was any different than he had been. He saw His body in the proper perspective.

Jesus continued His walk on this earth in obedience to His Father. Matthew, Chapter 26, verse 39 says,

"And he went a little farther, and fell on His face, and prayed, saying, O my Father, if it is possible, let this cup pass from me: nevertheless not as I will, but as thou wilt."

He chose obedience as he was facing separation from His Father, and was willing to die in our stead which allowed the fulfilling of the scriptures.

For obedience, he received a seat at the right hand of the throne of God, where God has magnified His Word above all His name. (Ref. Psalm 138:2) Moreover, Philippians 2: 9-11 KJV, states how Jesus' perfect obedience brought Him great honor for His sacrifice.

"Wherefore God also hath highly exalted Him, and given Him a name which is above every name: That at the name of Jesus every knee should bow, of things in heaven, and things in earth, and things under the earth; And that every tongue should confess that Jesus Christ is Lord, to the glory of God the Father." Hallelujah!

How Much Does God Love Us-?

God's love for us, and the obedience of Jesus Christ was our saving grace. John 3:16 KJV says,

"For God so loved the world that he gave His only begotten Son, that whosoever believeth in Him should not perish, but have everlasting life."

Jesus did not have to go to the cross for us. He too had a choice as He lived on the earth. He chose to be governed by the Spirit of His Father. God gave His Son Jesus that we might live. Jesus, in obedience to his Father's will, gave His life for you and me. He took on all the sins of the world and died a painful, shameful, death, and went to hell in our stead, as a man that had sinned in every way. Death and destruction was his reward, and hell became His home. (Ref. Isaiah 54:7) Sin had a price tag attached to it. Only Jesus could pay.

"For the wages of sin is death, but the gift of God is eternal life through Jesus Christ our Lord."(Rom. 6:23)

There was hell to pay. Sin had a price and Jesus paid it. He came from heaven to earth, and from earth to hell. From heaven, where His totality was pure love (power) and righteousness; to earth, where he put on flesh made from the dust of the ground, (subjected to otherwise domination), and yet remained sinless. Then from earth to hell in all of its deceit and impurity.

Jesus paid it all! And became the savior of the world. Colossians 2:13-15 says,

"And you, being dead in your sins and the uncircumcision of your flesh, hath He quickened (made alive) together with Him, having forgiven you all trespasses; Blotting out the handwriting of ordinances that was against us, which was contrary to us, and took it out of the way, nailing it to His cross; And having spoiled principalities and powers, He made a show of them openly, triumphing over them in it." Hallelujah!

The Ultimate Sacrifice

Jesus took on my sin and gave me His truth. He took on my poverty and gave me His wealth. Jesus took on my sadness, my depression, my distress, and gave me His joy. He took on my rags and gave me His robe.

My spirit groaned, the least I could do is to put it on and wear it. Wear the robe, that I might see myself as a daughter of God Almighty. That I might know that the greater one lives in me. That I might realize I am the righteousness of God, not because of me, but because of Christ.

I receive you, Lord, as Lord. I welcome you. I love you. I trust you. I thank you for the ultimate sacrifice of your life that you gave for me.

Now Lord, what must I do?

Now that I have your truth, wealth, joy, divine health, as well as your robe, what must I do? I am wearing your robe. Along with everyone else that has accepted you as his Lord and Savior. We are the Body of Christ. The Church and we are wearing the King's robe. We have been put right back to where we were at the beginning.

"So God created human beings in His own image, in the image of God he created them; male and female he created them. And God blessed them, and said, "Be fruitful and multiply. Fill the earth and govern it. Reign over the fish in the sea, and over the birds in the sky, and all the animals that scurry along the ground." Genesis 1:27-28 NLT

The responsibility of this earth is in the hands of the people of God. Through Christ, we have all that we need to carry out the order of God. We are wearing the King's robe. By faith, we can operate in the King's name, while here on the earth. This is how we can conquer all the ills of this world. Through Christ, by faith; not through world systems which shall surely fail.

Water Baptism And Holy Spirit Baptism

John baptized Jesus of the water, as was deemed right and necessary by God at that time. Before Jesus came, many others were baptized in water by John. This was the order of God. During that particular dispensation of time called "the law," the water was quickened or made alive by God. Upon being baptized, people were truly washed from their sins and became new by calling on the name of the Lord. (Ref. Acts 22:16; John 3:5)

First John, Chapter 5, verses 4-8 says, "For whatsoever is born of God overcometh the world: and this is the victory that overcometh the world, even our faith. Who is he that overcometh the world, but he that believeth that Jesus is the Son of God? This is he that came by water and by blood, even Jesus Christ; not by water only, but by water and blood. And it is the Spirit that beareth witness because the Spirit is truth.

For there are three that bear record in heaven, the Father, the Word, and the Holy Ghost: and these three are one. And there are three that bear witness in earth, the spirit, and the water, and the blood: and these three agree in one."

If we look deeply into this, we can see the three dispensations of time that God designed for the earth.

The Father represents the period, where the will of God for the earth was to abide by the law. There were people on the earth who were not law-abiding. The Bible calls them Gentiles. The law-abiding people were the Jews. The Bible calls the Jews God's chosen people, however, God had plans for the Gentiles all along. God used the Apostle Paul to teach the Gentiles of their sonship rights along with the Jews. Let's read that.

Ephesians, Chapter 3, verses 6-9 says, "That the Gentiles shall be fellow heirs, and of the same body, and partakers of His promise in Christ by the gospel: Whereof, I was made a minister, according to the gift of the grace of God given unto me by the effectual working of His power. Unto me, who am less than the least of all saints, is this grace given, that I should preach among the Gentiles the unsearchable riches of Christ; And to make all men see what is the fellowship of the mystery, which from the beginning of the world hath been hidden in God, who created all things by Jesus Christ."

The Apostle Paul is saying that he is less than the least of all saints because he persecuted the church, and that his entire ministry was built upon the grace of God. He was called to the ministry to preach unto the Gentiles; that they may know that God had hidden within Himself, even from the beginning of the world that they would be equal with the Jews, and therefore able to receive the blessing of Abraham, as recorded in Galatians 3:14, "That the blessing of Abraham might come on the Gentiles through Jesus Christ; that we might receive the promise of the Spirit through faith." This blessing is righteousness by faith in Christ, which means through Christ, every curse of the old covenant has been removed, and every promise has been given.

The Word represents the period that Jesus, or the Word of God, became flesh and walked among men. This was necessary for the fulfilling of "The Law." All humans had sinned, and the wages of sin is death. (Ref. Rom. 6:23) So Jesus came, but that 'the gift of God is eternal life through Jesus Christ our Lord." Had not Jesus come to the earth, there would not be life on the earth. This dispensation is called "The Church."

During that short dispensation, Jesus set up the church. He taught his disciples and the people in the synagogues how life was to be lived on earth. The law structure of the first dispensation was no more. The laws of Moses were no longer the abiding order, which was held dear by the Jews however, the laws of God, which existed before the laws of Moses continued in existence. Am I saying the ten commandments are no longer necessary on the earth? No, however, I am saying since the coming of Christ Jesus, all of the law has been fulfilled as stated in Matthew 22:35-40.

In Matthew 22, verses 35 through 40, one of the Pharisees tried to trap Jesus with a particular question. He asked him, "Teacher, which is the most important commandment in the law of Moses?" Jesus replied, 'You must love the Lord your God with all your heart, all your soul, and all your mind.' This is the first and greatest commandment. A second is equally important: 'Love your neighbor as yourself.' The entire law and all the demands of the prophets are based on these two commandments." During the "Church" dispensation, Jesus introduced the greatest commandment which is love. These two commandments were to bring together the Jews and the Gentiles into one thought, through Christ Jesus, and eliminate all of the laws of rule-keeping and ceremonial washing of pots and cups that existed through the laws of Moses. As well as other laws that were not centered around love.

The "Holy Spirit" represents this present time, where God has poured out of His Spirit upon all flesh. This dispensation started on "The Day of Pentecost." God declares in the book of Acts, that these are the last days. We need God's Spirit, the Holy Spirit to live inside of us, to keep us, guide us, comfort us, love us, and correct us. Receiving the Spirit is a deliberate act on the part of the believer. He must be obtained by faith. This dispensation is called "Grace." Grace is Christ. And through Christ, every believer has been brought back to God as it was before the fall of humankind. Death has been conquered, and life on the other side of the cross is now available to all believers. Only life where there is rest, peace, love, joy, and prosperity through faith in Christ Jesus, our Lord.

1st John, 5:8 says, "And there are three that bear witness in earth, the spirit, and the water, and the blood; and these three agree in one."

The bible declares that Jesus Christ came by water and blood. We know that as John baptized Jesus, Luke 3:22 says,

"And the Holy Ghost descended in a bodily shape like a dove upon Him, and a voice came from heaven, which said, Thou art my beloved Son; in thee, I am well pleased."

Now Jesus was also of water and Spirit.

Luke 4:1, says, "And Jesus being full of the Holy Ghost returned from Jordan, and was led by the Spirit into the wilderness."

Water and Spirit were both necessary to bring together as "one" in Himself, all who were baptized of water, and all who are baptized of the Holy Spirit.

Now, during this dispensation of "Grace," we understand that water baptism is symbolic only, as opposed to the days of The Law, where the water was necessary. (Ref. Matt. 3:5-6) Water baptism is a wonderful outward statement for the new convert, such as rings at a wedding ceremony are given but are not necessary for the marriage to be honored. Water baptism is not necessary for a believer to be born again, because the commitment takes place in the heart. Many ceremonies are demonstrative and symbolic, making an outward statement of an inward commitment.

The coming of Jesus brought all people together as one in Him, which was God's plan all along. Jesus came to level the playing field. All people that have ever existed, and will exist, are all equal in Christ Jesus. Whether water, spirit, or blood, all have been connected through Christ Jesus, through all three dispensations of time on the earth.

Galatians 3: 26-29 NLT "For you are all children of God through faith in Christ Jesus. And all who have been united with Christ in baptism have put on Christ, like putting on new clothes. There is no longer Jew or Gentile, slave or free, male and female. For you are all one in Christ Jesus. And now that you belong to Christ, you are the true children of Abraham. You are his heirs, and God's promise to Abraham belongs to you."

The Day Of Pentecost

Acts, Chapter 2, verses 1-4 says, "And when the day of Pentecost was fully come, they were all with one accord in one place. And suddenly there came a sound from heaven as of a rushing mighty wind, and it filled all the house where they were sitting. And there appeared unto them cloven tongues like as of fire, and it sat upon each of them. And they were all filled with the Holy Ghost, and began to speak with other tongues, as the Spirit gave them utterance."

This was the beginning of the last days. The law needed to be fulfilled, and Jesus was the fulfillment.

Acts, Chapter 2, verses 5-8 says, "And there were dwelling at Jerusalem Jews, devout men, out of every nation under heaven. Now when this was noised abroad, the multitude came together and was confounded, because every man heard them speak in his own language. And they were all amazed and marveled, saying one to another, Behold, are not all these which speak Galilaeans? And how hear we every man in our own tongue, wherein we were born?"

This is the power of God and the wonderful works of the Holy Spirit. Since the arrival of the Holy Spirit on the earth, many believers have received Hirn, and have spoken in tongues as the Spirit gave them utterance.

Before Christ came, the people of God lived by the law. They governed their bodies after the laws of God. The Spirit had not yet come. After Christ rose from the dead and ascended back to the Father, all the law was fulfilled. Upon Christ's arrival, he sent the Holy Spirit to the earth. Now the people of God enjoy the indwelling of the Holy Spirit inside of them who leads and guides them from their insides outward. Our bodies are no longer the focus. The receiving of the Holy Spirit is what is necessary now to keep us. As our mind and our body is governed by the Spirit, we will be able to walk and live in the peace of God. Upon receiving Him, we will receive power. (Acts 1:8) This power is what causes believers to operate in life supernaturally. Also, the Holy Spirit enables us to speak in other tongues. These tongues in prayer are necessary to draw out wisdom from our spirits, into our natural lives. A gift from God to the believer that cannot be interpreted or interfered with by the enemy of God.

On the Day of Pentecost when all of the Jews, devout men out of every nation under heaven were gathered and heard all of their languages being spoken from whence they were born, they were amazed. This was not amazing because they spoke, this was amazing because they were understood. Had not anyone understood, what would have been the point? They could have said that Peter and the others were just making noise. They could have believed they were drunken as was insinuated in Acts, Chapter 2, verses

13. This was God! This was miraculous! Peter and the others were filled with the Spirit and began to speak in languages they had not learned. They were simply trusting God to do what Jesus had taught them during his time on the earth. They spoke, and the men from every nation under heaven heard them, and were amazed! This is the power of God!

Acts, Chapter 2, verses 9-11 says, "Parthians, and Medes, and Elamites, and the dwellers in Mesopotamia, and in Judaea, and Cappadocia, in Pontus, and Asia, Phrygia, and Pamphylia, in Egypt, and the parts of Libya about Cyrene, and strangers of Rome, Jews and proselytes, Cretes and Arabians, we do hear them speak in our tongues the wonderful works of God."

Out of their mouths came perfect praise. There were no repetitions of prayer which had been done in the synagogues; that was described in Matthew, Chapter 6. I can imagine what a wonderful time in the Lord was that day. This was the beginning of the church. The church that Christ will come back for. They were obedient, powerful, full of love and life, and with great manifestations of God.

Unfortunately today, many churches, (local assemblies) have no resemblance to the power and manifestations of God. They have no idea of what the receiving of the Holy Spirit is for. Without the leadership of the Holy Spirit, the local assembly makes up its own rules. It is guided in its own way. The book of Proverbs, Chapter 14, verses 12 says,

"There is a way that seemeth right unto a man, but the end thereof are the ways of death."

The Church is the Body of Christ. The purpose of His Body has already been established by God.

Acts, Chapter 2, verses 12-14 says, "And they were all amazed, and were in doubt, saying one to another, What meaneth this? Others mocking said, These men are full of new wine. But Peter, standing up with the eleven, lifted up his voice, and said to them, ye men of Judaea, and all ye that dwell at Jerusalem, be this known unto you, and hearken to my words:"

At this point, Peter began to preach a sermon that the power of God filled. Acts, Chapter 2, verses 15-18 Peter preached,

"For these are not drunken, as ye suppose, seeing it is but the third hour of the day. But this is that which was spoken by the prophet Joel, And it shall come to pass in the last days, saith God, I will pour out of my Spirit upon all flesh: and your sons and your daughters shall prophesy, and your young men shall see visions, and your old men shall dream dreams; And on my servants and on my handmaidens I will pour out in those days of my Spirit, and they shall prophesy:"

The prophet Joel had already prophesied about the last days. God had previously told Joel about the outpouring of His Spirit upon all flesh. God's plan has been set in order since before the world began. He loves us. The outpouring of His Spirit upon us is the gift of God. for whosoever will receive Him.

Acts, Chapter 2, verses 36-39 says,

"Therefore let all the house of Israel know assuredly, that God hath made that same Jesus, whom you have crucified, both Lord and Christ. Now when they heard this, they were pricked in their heart, and said unto Peter and to the rest of the apostles, Men, and brethren, what shall we do? Then Peter said unto them, Repent, and be baptized every one of you in the name of Jesus Christ for the remission of sins, and ye shall receive the gift of the Holy Ghost. For the promise is unto you, and to your children, and to all that are afar off, even as many as the Lord our God shall call."

Christ Is The Fulfillment

Jesus Christ is Lord! He is the totality of our livelihood. He is the reason we have life. He is the reason for every season. Without Him, without the sacrifice of His life; death, hell, and the grave would have won, we would all be dead (spiritually) and eventually, physically. Sin would rule, and hell would be our eternal home.

All things have been fulfilled in Christ.

Colossians 2: 9-10, "For in Him dwelleth all the fullness of the Godhead bodily. And ye are complete in Him, which is the head of all principality and power:"

Galatians 5: 1, "Stand fast therefore in the liberty wherewith Christ hath made us free, and be not entangled again with the yoke of bondage."

Galatians 5: 14, "For all the law is fulfilled in one word, even in this, Thou shalt love thy neighbor as thyself."

Ephesians 3: 19, "And to know the love of Christ, which passeth knowledge, that ye might be filled with all the fullness of God."

Matthew 5: 17-18, "Think not that I am come to destroy the law or the prophets: I am not come to destroy, but to fulfill. For verily I say unto you, till heaven and earth pass, one jot or one tittle shall in no wise pass from the law, till all be fulfilled."

All have been fulfilled in Christ Jesus. Everything that exists is now made new. We are nothing in ourselves, but in Christ we are complete. We have no need. We have no want. We have no lack in Christ. His reason for coming was that man might be saved through His sacrifice. Now after perfect obedience to His Father, Christ hath made us free. (Ref. Gal. 5:1)

We are subject to none. We are in bondage to none. We are free. All who have received Christ are now free. There is nothing that can hold us fast. We are the greatest of God's creations on the earth. We have been instructed to have dominion over the earth. We have been instructed to be fruitful, to multiply, to replenish, and to subdue the earth. (Ref. Gen. 1:28)

To have dominion means to rule. God's instructions for mankind was to have dominion over all fish, fowl, cattle, the earth, and every creeping thing that creepeth upon the earth, not each other. In the book of Genesis where it talks about all of the animals, fowl, and fish, that God made, it says He made them all from the earth and water. The earth and water can be dominated. Human beings are spirits that live in a body and possess a soul. The spirit of a man cannot be dominated. No human can dominate the spirit that God put in another human. However, the body can be dominated, because it was made from the dust of the ground. The body is bought and sold sometimes like property. However, God never intended for this to be so. He gave dominion over the earth to humankind, which includes males and females.

I have heard said that God was not talking to the female when he instructed them to have dominion. I guess they have never read Genesis, Chapter 1, verses 27-28, which includes females. The earth was made to be ruled, and God put human beings in charge. Certainly, a woman can buy and sell a property just like a man. A woman can own cattle, or catch a fish, just like a man. God is not concerned with such small-minded matters. All things have been fulfilled in Christ. He is the fulfillment! All eyes should be on Him, not us. Anytime we find ourselves giving thought to other people, and saying what we think they can and cannot do in God, our focus is in the wrong place. Nothing is because of men, or women, but because of Jesus Christ. He died for humankind, not me or you. And according to Romans, Chapter 8, verse 34, He is risen again, and is even at the right hand of God, making intercession for us.

That kind of thinking exists because people are power-hungry, and as a result, they attempt to exclude others. As well as the thinking that there are limited resources in the world, and it is simply not so. There is an order that God set in place for men and women, but which one has dominion over cattle, birds, and fish has nothing to do with it.

God continues His instruction for us to be fruitful and multiply. When we are in Christ, everything we put our hands to should prosper. The Apostle Paul wrote in the third chapter of his letter to the Ephesians, that if we know and have the love of Christ, we have better than knowledge. And because of that love, we are filled with all of the fullness of God. What powerful beings we must be, to have all of the fullness of God within us. Therefore being fruitful, and multiplying should come relatively naturally for people of God. Increasing in the kingdom is what God expects from us.

Then He says for us to replenish and subdue the earth. He wants us to shower it with the goodness of God, as we walk knowing everything is subject unto us. Psalms 37:18-19 says,

"The Lord knoweth the days of the upright: and their inheritance shall be forever. They shall not be ashamed in the evil time: and in the days of famine they shall be satisfied."

God has made provision for the earth. Even in times of famine, He says the righteous shall be satisfied. He has given specific instructions on living according to His ways.

Matthew, Chapter 22, verses 37-40, one of the Pharisees asked Jesus which is the great commandment in the law?

"Jesus said unto him, Thou shalt love the Lord thy God with all thy heart, and with all thy soul, and with all thy mind. This is the first and great commandment. And the second is like, unto it, Thou shalt love thy neighbor as thyself. On these two commandments hang all the law and the prophets."

Jesus declares that when we love God with our entire being and love our neighbors as ourselves, all the law and all the prophets are taken care of. Christ is the fulfillment! It is finished.

After giving our lives to God, through Christ, loving Him with our all, and our neighbors as ourselves, we are the people whom He trusts to rule the earth that He created, made, and loved.

A Revelation Of God's Finished Work

Anyone who thinks God is still working has not the revelation. Anyone who is waiting on God to do something in his life has not the revelation. Anyone who says, "God is not finished with me yet," has not the revelation. Anyone who is just waiting on God has not the revelation.

In the book of Genesis, Chapter 2, verses 1-3 says, "Thus the heavens and the earth were finished, and all the host of them. And on the seventh day, God ended his work which he had made; and He rested on the seventh day from all His work which He had made. And God blessed the seventh day, and sanctified it: because that in it He had rested from all His work which God created and made."

Once we understand God in His infinite wisdom, and His creative and perfect faith, does not do anything partially, but completely, we will then understand that we, His creation, are complete, entire, and wanting nothing.

If we could open our minds to know that God is subject to no limitations, that He extends indefinitely. And that His immeasurable, inconceivable, greatness is us, and all the worlds around us. Only then could we begin to recognize our greatness, therefore our ability to heal the world. We are not waiting on God, he is waiting on us!

In the book of Hebrews, Chapter 12, verses 1-2, the writer gives us this beautifully written instruction on living in our entirety.

"Wherefore seeing we are also compassed about with so great a cloud of witnesses, let us lay aside every weight, and the sin which doth so easily beset us, and let us run with patience the race that is set before us, Looking unto Jesus the author and finisher of our faith; who for the joy that was set before Him endured the cross, despising the shame, and is set down at the right hand of the throne of God."

Because of Jesus, who has redeemed us, purchased us, and brought us back to God, we are back to where we were in the beginning. Now, through faith in Christ Jesus, we are complete.

Verse 2 above says Jesus is the author and finisher of our faith, which means, He is the beginning and the ending of our faith. Jesus is it. We are complete in Him. There is no waiting on God to get finished. God is already finished. Everything about us and all of creation is finished, beautiful, and wonderful. And that's God! We have the choice to believe it and receive it. Once we do that, we'll start walking in it.

A Revelation Of God's Order For The Family

Genesis, Chapter 2, verses 24-25 says, "Therefore shall a man leave his father and his mother, and shall cleave unto his wife: and they shall be one flesh. And they were both naked, the man and his wife, and were not ashamed."

Here God's instructions are directed to a man. If you have become a man, God says for you to leave your father and your mother, take a wife and cleave unto her, be one flesh, be naked, and be not ashamed with her.

If you have not become a man, do none of the above.

First, let's look at how God defines a man. We realize the word man is inclusive of the entire human being species that God created. However, in verses 24 and 25, He was talking to the male.

In Genesis, Chapter 1, verses 26-28 says, "And God said, Let us make man in our image, after our likeness: and let them have dominion over the fish of the sea, and over the fowl of the air, and over the cattle, and over all the earth, and over every creeping thing that creepeth upon the earth. So God created man in His own image, in the image of God created He him; male and female created He them. And God blessed them, and God said unto them, Be fruitful and multiply, and replenish the earth, and subdue it: and have dominion over the fish of the sea, and over the fowl of the air, and over every living thing that moveth upon the earth. "

The word image comes from a word that means class, the God class, unlike all the other animal beings God created and made. He created and made humans after the likeness of himself, respectively being three in one. Consisting of God the Father, Jesus the Son, and the Holy Spirit. The three agree in one. We are also triune beings, consisting of spirit, soul, and body. When operated properly, the three agree in one and can fulfill the extraordinary human experience God desired for humankind. (Ref. 1st Thess. 5:23)

God created humankind to be responsible. In the spirit part of the human, God wants humans to respond to Him; to acknowledge Him in all of his ways. To respond to his spirituality, that he may recognize the greater one inside of him. Acknowledging God, the creator, and being led by his spirit will cause a human being to live out this life on top, as well as cause a man to correctly lead his family, that harmony will exist in the household.

In the soul of a human, meaning his mind, his will, his emotions, his imagination, and his intellect; God wants a human to respond to His ways. While instructing the male, He wants him to allow his thought patterns to be governed after Him, and His divine order of prosperity and abundance. Which would, in turn, result in total provision for the family "from God," not from the man.

In his body, God wants a man to respond to His order for keeping himself. Never overindulging the body in anything. But being mindful of the several members of the body, and all of the different functions necessary to keep it.

Considering God instructed the man to take a wife and become one flesh with her, simply means God is holding the man responsible for the one body that they have become. Remember, they are one flesh. God will not hold one person responsible for what another person does. After marriage, God sees the two people as one person. Regardless of how we see it. Regardless of how agreeable the marriage may or may not be. When He looks at the married, he sees one person.

Therefore if you are a male, and you are able and willing to respond to God in every way. As well as becoming one flesh with your wife, taking full responsibility for the one flesh, God says you are a man. The man is who God holds responsible for the one flesh, however, He encourages both the husband and the wife to submit to one another. This is marriage designed by God. He has set an order by which a family should live to maintain peace and harmony. This can be referenced in Ephesians 5:21-28 The Message Translation. Let's read it.

"Out of respect for Christ, be courteously reverent to one another. Wives, understand and support your husbands in ways that show your support for Christ. The husband provides leadership to his wife the way Christ does to his church, not by domineering but by cherishing. So just as the church submits to Christ as he exercises such leadership, wives should likewise submit to their husbands. Husbands, go all out in your love for your wives, exactly as Christ did for the church- a love marked by giving, not getting. Christ's love makes the church whole. His words evoke her beauty. Everything he does and says is designed to bring the best out of her, dressing her in dazzling white silk, radiant with holiness. And that is how husbands ought to love their wives. They're really doing themselves a favor- since they're already "one" in marriage."

This is the set order given by God, and it works beautifully when operated properly. As with our physical bodies, our hands, feet, legs, and so forth do not do anything without the consent of our head. Our head is always over our body, even literally. When our head is operating properly, and our mind is sound and thinking clearly, our body will never be out of order. Our feet will never go before our head gives the instruction. This is why husbands are instructed to love their wives, even as Christ loves the church, and gave himself for it. Through love the wife is comfortable in knowing her "body" is under the authority and protection of her husband. Her spirit is given to Christ, and her soul is her responsibility. To love like Christ is a great responsibility, and it is necessary to operate this principle properly.

God's order is wonderful and powerful. Show me a man that honors his wife, and I'll show you the most orderly and submitted couple you have ever seen. If you are a man of God, and you have a wife that you love and cleave to, as God instructed, you will in turn have a happy and satisfied wife, you will be blessed. And your prayers will not be hindered. (Ref, 1Peter 3:7)

Moreover, God gave the woman to Adam to be a help or a blessing to him. Some men do not see their wives as such. The bible calls this blessing a helper just right for Adam. They were one in spirit, and one in the flesh until God removed a rib and made the body of the woman. Now, Adam was no longer alone or all in one. They were one spirit yet in two individual bodies. This way one could help the other. Many husbands are not willing to admit that they need help, (more spiritual than natural) just as many wives will say they do not need their husband to be the head over their body, or the one flesh, however, both are under the order of God.

Being that Christ is the head of the church, the female's spirit is not subject to her husband, but unto Christ. He is the head of that body, which is the Body of Christ, or The Church.

As God, His Son, and His Spirit are one, they agree. Do not allow Satan to separate your oneness in Christ. When husbands and or wives see their spouse as a separate person from themselves, it gives place to Satan to pit one against the other. As they both commit to submitting to their spirit, which are plugged into the Holy Spirit, their spirit, soul, and body will work together in agreement. Hold on tightly to each other and live the life of faith!

"Be Strong In The Lord"

A young lady came to me one day, worn out with a problem, and insistent upon giving up. I was given a word to give to her right then that has since meant so much to me.

She said to me, "It's hard being strong all the time."

I said to her, "It is hard being strong if you're weak. But it's not hard being strong if you're strong. And that, my sister, is a choice." And I went on to teach this lesson:

Based upon Ephesians, Chapter 6, verse 10, "…be strong in the Lord, and the power of His might."

The Apostle Paul was talking to the church at Ephesus, and to the faithful in Christ Jesus. He simply says, "be strong." He goes on to tell them how and what they should do to continue in strength. Then in verses 13 and 14, he says, "Wherefore take unto you the whole armor of God that ye may be able to withstand in the evil day, and having done all to stand. Stand therefore, having your loins girt about with truth…"

After you have done all that you can do to stand, he simply says just keep standing. We can put on the Word of God, and wear it like clothing. After all, it is our protection.

I continued to Joshua, for the bible says: Out of the mouth of two witnesses:

Joshua, Chapter 1, verse 9..." Be strong and of good courage; be not afraid, neither be thou dismayed: for the Lord thy God is with thee whithersoever thou goest."

Knowing that you are not alone and that God is always with you, you can stand strong in total dependence on Him.

Deciding to be strong is a great choice! And you can live there by the strength of your mind.

A Thought For Christians Who Continue To Struggle With The Offenses Of Satan

A Christian who often struggles with the offenses of Satan is likely to wear more than one face. Regardless of one's profession of victory, our lives are our greatest testimony. If we are honest with ourselves, we know whether we have allowed ourselves to become offended or not. If so, we should ask ourselves this question:

Why am I offended, except that I lack the faith to believe?

Luke, Chapter 17, verse 1, Jesus says, "Then said He unto the disciples, it is impossible but that offenses will come: but woe unto him, through whom they come!"

Jesus was telling the disciples that offenses will come, and He went on to tell the fate of the one bringing the offense. Offenses will come, however, you don't have to be offended. Something may occur that is bothersome, but you don't have to be bothered.

These are choices we can make, upon recognition. We should recognize that offenses will come, but to be offended is not faith. Something bothersome may happen, but to be bothered is not faith. At these times, we can choose to rest in the love of God through Christ Jesus, knowing our Father is always with us, and there is nothing bigger than God.

Romans, Chapter 14, verse 23 says "...for whatsoever is not of faith is sin." Staying in the love of God, and not allowing ourselves to be moved by outside circumstances will help to keep us in faith.

In the amplified version of Luke, Chapter 17, verse 1, Jesus says, "...Temptations, (snares, traps set to entice to sin) are sure to come..." Offenses are coming to entice you to sin, and when you take the bait and become offended, you have been enticed, and sin is inevitable.

Hebrews, Chapter 11, verse 6 says, "But without faith, it is impossible to please Him: for- he that cometh to God must believe that He is and that He is a re-warder of them that diligently seek Him.

We should always stay in faith, that we might please God. Start to make faith confessions aloud in your hearing. This is always a good idea because it builds our faith.

"For as the rain comes down, and the snow from heaven, And do not return there, But water the earth, And make it bring forth and bud, That it may give seed to the sower And bread to the eater, So shall my word be that goes forth from My mouth; It shall not return to Me void, But it shall accomplish what I please, And it shall prosper in the thing for which I sent it." Isaiah 55:10-11 NKJV

I thank you Father, that just like the rain and snow don't go back up without watering the earth and causing it to bring flowers, trees, fruits, and vegetation, your Word to me and about me will not return to you without it doing exactly what you said it would. I believe it and receive it. Amen.

"Therefore if any man is in Christ, he is a new creature: old things are passed away; behold, all things have become new." II Cor. 5:17 I thank you, Father, for my past is behind me, and I am now new in your eyes, so I am also new in mine, in the name of Jesus.

"Being confident of this very thing, that he which hath begun a good work in you will perform it until the day of Jesus Christ." Philippians 1:6

Father, I am certain that you have begun a good work in me, and I know you are going to finish it, in Jesus' name.

"For I am persuaded, that neither death, nor life, nor angels, nor principalities, nor powers, nor things present, nor things to come, nor height, nor depth, nor any other creature, shall be able to separate us from the love of God, which is in Christ Jesus our Lord." Rom. 8:38-39

I thank you, Father, that there is nothing that can cause you to not love me, so I believe you will help me when I call, in Jesus' name.

After a period of faith confessions aloud, you are back on top! Then you can say to yourself, I'm not bothered, I'm blessed!! After making your confessions, make your request known unto God, through prayer and supplication, with thanksgiving. (Ref. Philippians 4:6) Stand boldly before His throne as he instructed us to do. Why? Because we know we are the righteousness of God through Christ Jesus. It is our spiritual and responsible right to be there. Putting off the struggles, and putting on strength, that we may continue in his service. (Ref. Heb. 4:16, 2 Cor. 5:21)

God Is A Great God

The prophet Isaiah records in the sixth chapter of his book a vision he saw. Verses 1-7:

"In the year that King Uzziah died I saw also the Lord sitting upon a throne, high and lifted up, and his train filled the temple. Above it stood the seraphim: each one had six wings; with twain, he covered his face, and with twain, he covered his feet, and with twain, he did fly. And one cried unto another, and said, Holy, holy, holy, is the Lord of host: the whole earth is full of his glory. And the post of the door moved at the voice of him that cried, and the house was filled with smoke. Then said I, Woe is me! For I am undone; because I am a man of unclean lips, and I dwell among a people of unclean lips: for mine eyes have seen the King, the Lord of hosts. Then flew one of the seraphim unto me, having a live coal in his hand, which he had taken with the tongs from off the altar: And he laid it upon my mouth, and said, Lo, this hath touched thy lips; and your iniquity is taken away, and thy sin purged."

God is a great God! He is not small and limited to earthly matters. He is forever. The prophet Isaiah says he saw Him high and lifted up. The seraphim (which are God's angels) declare that the whole earth is full of His glory.

Isaiah tells of a time in his mind, he was not prepared for the presence of God to visit him. God saw things differently. God does not look upon our bodies as being who we are. Fortunately, He looks at our hearts. God knew Isaiah, and Isaiah knew God, otherwise, he could not have recognized His presence through vision.

What many people call, "a calling" from God, I believe happens before birth, simply because we were spirit beings with God, long before we were born to our parents. This belief is based upon Jeremiah, Chapter 1, verses 4-5, it reads,

''Then the word of the Lord came unto me saying, Before I formed thee in the belly, I knew thee; and before thou camest forth out of the womb, I sanctified thee, and I ordained thee a prophet unto the nations.''

The called ones are many times adults before they're ready and He commissions them to go out, but according to Jeremiah, the calling or assignment happens well before birth.

The prophet Isaiah already knew God, and at the presence of God, he immediately began to confess that he was undone. He said, "Woe is me! For I am undone; because I am a man of unclean lips, and I dwell among a people of unclean lips…" He didn't start telling God what all good deeds he had done, he confessed that he was a man of unclean lips. 1st John, Chapter 1, verse 9 says,

"If we confess our sin, he is faithful and just to forgive us our sin, and to cleanse us from all unrighteousness."

God is a great God! Upon our confession, His forgiveness and cleansing are immediate. Then through obedience to His Word, we are ready to be used.

Isaiah, Chapter 6, verses 8-9 says, "Also I heard the voice of the Lord, saying, whom, shall I send, and who will go for us? Then said I, Here am I; send me. And He said, Go, and tell this people, Hear ye indeed, but understand not; see ye indeed, but perceive not."

We can see where God commissioned Isaiah to go out. Before his commission, God made Himself known unto Isaiah through vision. Isaiah then had an opportunity to confess, and allow the cleansing of his soul. Now he is ready to be used.

God is always orderly. There is an invitation by way of the Spirit, and response also by the Spirit, and then manifested into the working of the Kingdom of God.

God never commissions one, without also making the necessary provisions to do the work He has assigned. God's work is great, and God is a great God! Far too often people misrepresent God with their pitiful display of resources to do the Father's work. The same faith it took to receive and acknowledge the call, is the same faith needed to receive the provisions to carry it out. God is not dependent upon the people. He can raise the rocks in reverence to Him if He so desires. However, He desires obedient people that love Him. He will be to them a God of peace and abundance, and all of eternity will be the length of their days.

As I was writing, the voice of God came unto me saying, "This is the voice of God. I have called you, and you have not inclined your ear to me. All who are called of me, there are resources throughout the land. Seek ye me, and I will give it to you. Feed the people my Word, and I will feed them bread."

I stood up from my computer, somewhat stunned, not recognizing at the time that this was my commission. I sat back down, bowed my head, and talked to God. I believed as a child, that I had been called by God, but had not acknowledged it to anyone. At the time of this writing, I was in my early thirties. I knew then for sure but chose not to acknowledge it. At the time it seemed like every other female in the surrounding areas was announcing "a calling." I didn't want to be one in that number. I was soon after that sent (I believe by God,) to a correctional facility with a word for a release of an inmate. I went and spoke the word to him inside the facility. His wife called and said he had been released before sunup the next morning. A few years later he became a pastor and is pastoring today. I have since learned to be obedient, as well as quick to respond to the promptings of the Spirit, regardless of how some things may seem to me.

Receiving Faith

Romans 10:17 "So then faith cometh by hearing, and hearing by the Word of God."

In applying this verse to our lives, it is important to note the order of God. Hebrews 11:6 says,

"But without faith, it is impossible to please him: for he- that cometh to God must believe that he is and that he is a re-warder of them that diligently seek him."

Therefore faith is a great thing to obtain, and necessary to please God.

To hear the Word of God with our ears, and keep it there produces very little. Many have heard the Word of God for years, but their faith is yet undeveloped. Once you allow the Word to get on the inside of you, the power of the Word causes you to become stronger than you were before hearing it. This is how "faith cometh." We don't do anything other than receive the Word into our spirit. The seed of the Word will cause outward growth, from the spirit to the soul, and then to the body, faith comes.

The more faith used to believe the Word of God, the more faith comes for our use.

Romans 12:3b "…God hath dealt to every man the measure of faith."

We start off ahead. God has dealt the measure of faith to each of us. It's the same amount for each of us. It's up to us to develop it. The hearing with our ears happens in the same order, we just don't think about it. All of our senses are programmed to our understanding. There are many people without the use of their senses that can still understand what something feels like, or what something looks, smells, sounds, or tastes like. This is the power of God! He made us all with the ability to be overcomers regardless of our circumstances. This is an act of our will, which is one component of the soul. Our will for ourselves can supersede our physical body. This choice is a part of our inner being from the beginning.

In all of human history, you can find many people or cultures who willed themselves above circumstances that were even thought to be disabling. We can always choose. Our God-given choice is always present on the inside of us, keeping us in the hands of freedom. We are the creations of the Almighty God. We are brilliantly made and able.

Recognizing our creator, responding to Him with our spirit, soul, and body; living our lives according to His will, receiving His Word or truth into ourselves, causes us to mature spiritually. It takes faith. Our spirit is who we are. Many people go to great lengths to improve their bodies, not recognizing that a strong spirit is the main keeper and wellness of the body. It would be a great thing to strive in the maturing of our spirit, living by faith, which causes the soul and body to function properly.

Growing in faith pleases God. Because it says to Him that we trust Him. As we receive faith, we should use it to accomplish the things of God. Faith is power. It is what God used to bring this entire world into existence. He spoke the Word, mixed with faith, and that which was not present came into being. He declares unto us in Mark, chapter 11, that we can have whatsoever we say if we use faith properly. He says for us to:

"Have faith in God. For verily I say unto you, That whosoever shall say unto this mountain, Be thou removed, and be thou cast into the sea; and shall not doubt in his heart, but shall believe that those things which he saith shall come to pass; he shall have whatsoever he saith. Therefore I say unto you, what things soever ye desire, when ye pray, believe that ye receive them, and ye shall have them." (Mark 11: 22-24)

A Revelation From The Book Of Genesis

Genesis, Chapter 3, verse 8 says, "And they heard the voice of the Lord God walking in the garden in the cool of the day: and Adam and his wife hid themselves from the presence of the Lord God amongst the trees of the garden."

Many have read this passage and presumed God, was walking around in the garden, and Adam and Eve heard him coming. It reads, "And they heard the voice of the Lord God walking in the garden." Yes, God's voice was walking. His words were manifest and were walking upon the earth in the garden. God himself was not walking in the garden, but his voice was, which is Jesus Christ, the Word of God. It is further revealed that at this time when Adam and Eve were in trouble and had a need, Jesus was immediately present. He was there for their provision, but they were afraid because of their disobedience.

This is how the word became flesh, through faith. The actual voice of God became manifest. His voice was walking and talking and lived on the earth in the form of a human being called Jesus.

Perfected faith in the spoken word produces far more power than we realize.

This takes us to the book of John, Chapter 1, verses 1-4 says,

"In the beginning was the Word, and the Word was with God, and the Word was God. The same was in the beginning with God. All things were made by him, and without him was not anything made that was made. In him was life, and the life was the light of men."

Jesus was present in the beginning. The bible says, He was the Word, and the Word was with God, and the Word was God." They are one. We too are one with our word. Our word somewhere is just like we are there. Our words are important. They represent us in and out of our presence.

God is omniscient, meaning He is infinitely aware. He has universal knowledge. Science according to the earth's best scientist, is His footstool. God is omnipotent and omnipresent. He has unlimited authority and influence, and He is present in all places at all times.

His voice was heard by Adam and Eve in the garden. That does not mean His totality was in the garden as has been implied by some. The Godhead is not containable by any means.

God sent His Word to the earth, which is Jesus, whom the bible says is the same as God. After His Word fulfilled the law on the earth, He ascended and sent God's Spirit to the earth. He too is one with God. He is the Holy Spirit of God. He lives within every believer that has invited Him in. He will lead and guide you into all truth. We freely and willingly walk after Him, as he leads us from within. He is "I am." He is all!

He is eternity.

Obedient To The Spirit, Causes Prosperity In The Flesh

God's choice for man is for him to be empowered, blessed, and prosperous in every way. (Ref. Gen. 1:26-31)We are of God. We are spirit beings. Without Him, it is impossible to continue. God is a Spirit. When the spirit leaves the body, it is the equivalent of God's absence. Void of life. Void of breath.

3rd John, 1:2 says, "Beloved, I wish above all things that thou mayest prosper and be in health, even as thy soul prospereth."

The same verse in the paraphrased version says: "Dear friend, I am praying that all is well with you and that your body is as healthy as I know your soul is."

John is telling the church that it is his prayer that they prosper in all ways; including their spirit, soul, and body. Through this way, he would know that they were prospering in truth, which is the spirit, then outward. All prosperity of God happens in order. He is an orderly Father. Many times people heap up things for themselves, but it is not the prosperity of God.

Only when our spirit abides with the Spirit of God, does it manifest into our spirit being blessed, after which our soul, (sound mind) and then our body will follow thereafter in good health.

John continues in that chapter, verses 3-4, "For I rejoice greatly when the brethren came and testified of the truth that is in thee, even as thou walkest in the truth. I have no greater joy than to hear that my children walk in truth."

There is a spiritual order with which we should live if we desire to prosper and be in health. John was rejoicing over the truth, which is the same as the Spirit. (Ref. 1st John 5:6) As far as John was concerned, there was no explanation needed about anything he had taught. He knew that the Spirit was true, and if they lived their lives as he had taught them, it would cause them to be blessed. This would result in their soul or mind being sound and their body is in great health.

The orderly ways of God always produce manifold blessings. Many times people make excuses about their lives not lining up with the order and then say God told them to do something different. God will never tell us to do anything contrary to His Word. He, His Word, and His Spirit are one. They always agree. And choosing to put God and His ways first, will result in prosperity for us.

We are never without a choice. In Christ, there is freedom and free will. Therefore the Word says:

"Be not deceived; God is not mocked; for whatsoever a man soweth, that shall he also reap.

For he that soweth to his flesh shall of the flesh reap corruption, but he that soweth to the Spirit shall of the Spirit reap life everlasting." (Gal. 6:7-8)

You can choose God's way, or you can choose your way, and get the results that it brings. It's up to you.

Matthew, 6:33, Jesus says, "But seek ye first the kingdom of God and His righteousness, and all these things shall be added unto you."

This verse is informing us that to obtain prosperity, in life God's way, we must first seek God and His righteousness. Order is important to God. Whatever He says for us to do first, is the order with which we should follow to obtain His blessings, therefore enabling us to be a blessing to others.

Philippians 4:19 says, "But my God shall supply all your need according to His riches in glory by Christ Jesus."

Here the Apostle Paul was pastoring the church at Philippi. They had sent toward his personal need, continuing in tithes and offerings, even when he was teaching the Word in another country. They were faithful to God through His servant Paul. They believed in God, and they proved it with their actions. After which, they believed that God would then take action on their behalf, making sure that their need was met. God's giving is always bigger than ours. They came out on the better end. This happens according to one's level of faith and faithfulness to the Word of God.

God's provisions for us are made daily, over and over. Oftentimes, people don't recognize His hand. Depending on God for our needs is what we should do. Our working is for reasons above making money. Everything God instructs us to do has manifold blessings. After all, we are all blessed far beyond our knowledge, and the grace of God has given us far more than we could ever earn.

We should work simply because God instructed us to do so. He gave Adam the job of keeping the garden. Certainly, this garden was a blessing to more than just them. One state that the world is in is not realizing that they should seek God's ways, to prosper, that hunger and homelessness not abound. Satan has used a certain scripture to lure Christians away from prosperity thinking, that he can keep people poor, hungry, and out of doors. 1st Tim. 6:10 says,

"For the love of money is the root of all evil: which while some converted after, they have erred from the faith, and pierced themselves through with many sorrows."

This verse is talking about those who love money and will do anything to get it. Not the people of God, who are responsible for the upbuilding of God's Kingdom on earth. God declares that seeking Him first will cause His blessings to come to you. He wants us to be blessed financially, as well as in other ways, that we may be a blessing to others. Psalms 112: 1-3 says,

"Praise- ye the Lord. Blessed is the man that feareth the Lord that delighteth greatly in His commandments.

His seed shall be mighty upon earth: the generation of the upright shall be blessed. Wealth and riches shall be in his house: and his righteousness endureth forever."

These verses are clear. They say the man that fears the Lord is blessed, as he delights greatly in the Lord's commandments. It declares his seed or children will be mighty upon the earth for generations, through uprightness. The wealth and riches that are mentioned are physical, tangible things. 1st Tim. 6:17 says, "Charge them that are rich in this world, that they are not high minded, nor trust in uncertain riches, but in the living God, who giveth us richly all things to enjoy."

God admonishes the rich to not be high-minded because of riches, as well as instruction on recognizing that some riches are uncertain, meaning they are not from God. He says don't put your trust in them. The verse goes on to say trust in the living God, who gives us richly all things to enjoy. Trusting in God affirms our certainty that our riches are from Him, and will cause enjoyment.

These verses are wonderful promises of God. They are also conditioned upon the obedience of being given to God. Giving Him reverence. Obeying His order. Seeking Him and his righteousness first before anything and anyone else. He is all-knowing, all-loving, and all-forgiving. All greatness is because of Him. He wants us to come to Him, that he may direct our path. What a warm and wonderful Father we have.

Luke 12:48 says, "…For unto whomsoever much is given, of him shall be much required:"

God also requires things of us. He has made us responsible by giving us dominion over all the earth. He has set all provisions for our use. There is no lack in God, and there is no lack in His creation. We must first look to God, and live our lives in obedience to His Word. In turn, we can expect all of our needs to be met, to richly have things to enjoy, to have wealth and riches in our house, to have all these things added unto us, that we may continue in His service.

The Ability Of Prayer

On the offensive side, prayer can combat, and win over anything that is opposing. Prayer expels evil thoughts, as well as an undermining and spiritual capture of evil spiritual force.

On the defensive side, prayer individually, as well as collectively, is like a huge blanket of positive force that disallows the entrance of anything unlike itself. While in the meantime, its spiritual existence is lifting higher, always higher to a divine level that cannot be touched by anything lesser than itself.

When expressed from the spirit (heart) back to God, in the name of Jesus, (because God has magnified His Word above His name) (Psalms 138:2) the spoken word is more powerful than everything visible. It is able! It is more than enough! It is the very essence (power) of God!

Religion

Webster's dictionary defines religion as "the service or worship of God or the supernatural. A personal set or institutionalized system of religious attitudes, beliefs, and practices. Commitment or devotion to religious faith or observance."

As a child, I thought religion was directly and undoubtedly related to God. I later found out that religions, as the definition says, are a personal set, a religious attitude, or certain beliefs that are practiced. Therefore, I have concluded that since God is a Spirit, according to John 4:24, and personal sets, attitudes and certain practices happen in the mind; religion does not directly and undoubtedly relate to God. According to John 4:24, the only way to relate to God is through the Spirit, which is truth. (Ref. 1st John 5:6)

Religion, as practiced by some, does not line up with the New Testament Covenant of Jesus Christ, but is in direct proportion with the feelings of people, the religious attitudes, and many traditional practices. In this, it is clear that religion is not for those of us who have received Jesus Christ, as our savior.

We understand that our bodies are no longer the focus because we are not under the law. Therefore, our feelings and attitudes toward things are not what we should live by. It is the Spirit of God, who lives within us, and leads us from the inside outward. This is the order of God. The spirit, then the soul, and then the body. (Ref. 1st Thess. 5:23) The human being spirit that is given to the Holy Spirit leads and guides our soul, (mind) then our mind leads and guides our bodies. We need the Holy Spirit to lead and guide us by way of our spirit. Without the leadership of the Spirit, our minds could lead us anywhere. And for many people, their minds do, and not even recognize that they are off course.

Faith is necessary to receive the Holy Spirit after you have been born again. This is pleasing to God. (Ref. Heb. 11:6) It does not take faith to be committed to religious traditional practices, but it does take faith to please God. We must recognize the difference.

It does not matter how long, and with what great fervor and sincerity one does his traditional practices and programs. God is not involved in religious practices, which happen in the mind and the body. Religion has an appearance of good in the eyes of those who practice it. It allows people the ability to look upon themselves, as well as others, and decide whether they are godly or not by their appearance. People make themselves a judge in religion because they can look upon your outer self, and decide whether they think you have God or not.

God is not even present at this outside show. He is an inner man God, and by the Spirit only does he commune with humankind.

In the book of Colossians, the writer Paul was teaching the church at Colosse the differences in legalism, and God through Christ. The differences are vast. Unfortunately, many people see them as the same thing. They think keeping the laws of America is the same as being in the will of God. There are laws on the books of America, that according to the bible, God never intended for it to be so. God is not an American citizen. He does not adhere to America's laws. He is the creator and maker of the whole world. One of the most commonly known scriptures of all times is John 3:16. It says,

"For God so loved the world that He gave His only begotten Son, that whosoever believeth in Him should not perish, but have everlasting life."

This scripture says God gave His Son for the World. And the time for human beings to open themselves and reach across the world to one another is at hand. I read somewhere we don't all speak the same language, but we can all smile.

When we perceive God only as ourselves, and not see Him through Christ, according to the new covenant, we do ourselves a great disservice. The day that we all surrender, and allow our perception of God, and Jesus to be all things to all people will be a great day because they are anyway. And everyone who continues to try to keep others out, because of their own faithless, religious, ungodly attitudes, will find themselves living a life of despair, and after this life, in desperate need of a cool drink of water.

How Jesus looked when He walked on the earth had significance for that dispensation of time only. Everything since has been fulfilled. To be in the order of God now in this dispensation of Grace, is to walk in the spirit. It has no physical looks. What color is love? Which sex is faith? What race is hope?

1st Corinthians 13:13 says, "And now abideth faith, hope, charity, these three; but the greatest of these is charity."

We know that charity is love, and it happens on the inside.

The physical looks of a person mean nothing in the kingdom of God. Not race, sex, or any other physical aspects of our outer being. This is the time of the spirit. God is an awesome God. He does not do anything partially but completely. All of His creation is in the order with which He perfectly planned it.

The prophet Joel prophesied about a time when God would pour out of His Spirit upon all flesh. That time is now. The Spirit of God is the one that will distinguish who belongs to Him, and who does not. Skin color, sex, any or all outerwear, worn on our bodies have absolutely nothing to do with us belonging to God through Christ.

The bible talks very plainly about how Jesus went from country to country teaching, healing, loving them all equally, and having compassion towards them in need. Surely we know all the people were not all the same. As He crossed overseas doing His mighty works, teaching, and feeding multitudes at a time. Surely we know they did not all look alike.

Even for those who do not claim Jesus Christ, he loves them all the same. I have not studied all religions, however, the ones I have looked into seemed to say very little about the world at large. You have to be that particular race, or sex, or nationality to be an equal part. I know some will say with Jesus it is the same way. Well, not according to Jesus. Of course, some have tried to make Him out to be only for the ones who look like them.

These outer things once again are religious, but not godly. With any situation, once you get the truth, you can better understand its purpose. The bible says God gave His Son for the World.

Galatians 3: 26-28 says, "For ye are all the children of God by faith in Christ Jesus. For as many of you as have been baptized into Christ have put on Christ. There is neither Jew nor Greek, there is neither bond nor free, there is neither male nor female: for ye are all one in Christ Jesus."

This representation of Jews and Greeks, who were once separate, now stand together equally in Christ. The bond represented by Abraham's son, Ishmael, and the free, represented by Abraham's son Isaac, now stand together as one in Christ Jesus. The male and the female now stand together as one in Christ Jesus.

This represents the entire world of people. Many who were once outside of God's covenant has been brought back to God, through purchase, by the blood of Christ Jesus.

Galatians 3:29 says, "And if ye be Christ's, then are ye Abraham's seed, and heirs according to the promise."

Therefore, all who have received Christ Jesus are Abraham's seed and are entitled to the promise. This promise is righteousness. Having been made righteous, through Christ, not by any of our own doing, is the tie that binds the people of God into "One Holy Race." A race that is based upon our spirit, and not our physical body.

The essence of the promise is the blessing of Abraham, which is to be made righteous. All that was Abraham's is ours by inheritance. All curses that were once in operation, are no longer in operation.

Gal. 3:9-11 says, "So then they which be of faith are blessed with faithful Abraham. For as many as are of the works of the law are under the curse: for it is written, Cursed is every one that continueth not in all things which are written in the book of the law to do them. But that no man is justified by the law in the sight of God, it is evident: for, The just shall live by faith."

Christ is the head over all. (Ref. Ephesians 1:22) Only Christ can save us spiritually. Through Christ, we are all free. Everything has been fulfilled in Christ. He has extended Himself to all of the worlds. By faith, all can receive him.

Here again, our bodies and features, looks and sex is not the focus of "The Church" that Christ will come back for. These are all separation tactics people use out of fear, (many times unrecognized) to put themselves up ahead of someone else. They are religious nothings that God in his greatness could not care less about. It is the spirit of a human being that communes with God.

We should never focus on things that do not lead us in the direction of Christ. If we are being led by the Holy Spirit, we would not have that problem. Outside things, or things on or about the body, are not the focus of the Holy Spirit.

Mark 7:15 says, "There is nothing from without a man, that entering into him can defile him: but the things which come out of him, those are they that defile a man."

Proverbs 6:16-20 says, "These six things doth the Lord hate: yea, seven are an abomination unto Him: A proud look, a lying tongue, and hands that shed innocent blood, An heart that deviseth wicked imaginations, feet that be swift in running to mischief, A false witness that speaketh lies, and he that soweth discord among brethren. My son, keep thy father's commandment, and forsake not the law of thy mother."

These things come out of the heart, and God is not pleased. Religion tells us smoking, drinking, and sex, are the worse things a person can do. Of course, we should govern our mind and body after the Spirit, and we will control these things. In John, Chapter two, where Jesus turned water into wine at a wedding, certainly Jesus was not going against the order of God. And when the woman was caught in adultery, Jesus did not condemn her but told her to go and sin no more. (Ref. John 8:11) Before He came, the law was to stone her.

This is by no means encouraging smoking, drinking, fornication, or adultery, however, these things of the body were the focus of the "Law" period, before Christ. Now, all who are reborn through Christ Jesus, and walk after the Spirit, should renew their mind to the ways of Christ, which will in turn guide your body likewise. Our bodies are yet unredeemed. We have to work each day at bringing our bodies into subjection unto the Holy Spirit. (Read the book of Romans for these corrections.)

It is my conclusion then that religion as practiced in countless ways in this country, and throughout the world, is a false teacher. Strong, unchanging beliefs that are thought to be godly, but instead are made up of self-imposed religion. This is at least some of what the Apostle Paul was teaching the church at Colosse.

In Colossians 2:23, he says, "These things indeed have an appearance of wisdom in self-imposed religion, false humility, and neglect of the body, but are of no value against the indulgence of the flesh." (NKJV) He was letting them know that there was such a thing, and to be aware that it could lead them away from God. They thought in holding to these things, (outward things) they would become more godly. And these were the people who were considered the learned and teaching others.

Paul was warning people as far back as the first-century church, and he called it "self-imposed religion." A religion where people make the rules to suit themselves; adhere to them for long periods, passing them on for generations. After being held dear for so long, change is not welcome, and God is not recognized. However, the scriptures are no doubt used, just without being rightly divided, so that proper understanding would benefit lives. I would guess that there is much of this in every religion on the earth.

God is a Spirit. (John 4:24) He is not a religion. There is but one God. (1st Cor. 8:6) He created us all. He made us all, and He loves us all. Everything from Him will bless us. God is not mocked, (Gal. 6:7) and His Word is now! In Him, the end of everything is increasing. There is no death in Him. There is no poverty or sickness in Him. There is no homelessness, hunger, or disease in Him. He is the author of abundant life, and through Christ, we can all have Him. We should seek God first, (Matt 6:33) not religion. They are not the same. In choosing God, and His will for us, we choose life.

Jesus Christ, The Ultimate Authority And, "The Author Of Eternal Salvation"

Why is Jesus the ultimate authority, but that He served the most people? It is service that causes one to become authoritarian. To render service to your brother is what will cause him to look to you for advice. The service itself is what causes one to be put in this position. It does the lifting. It comes from the Spirit. To render or give to another person willingly, and generously comes from the spirit or heart of a man. This is the service of God.

In the book of John, Chapter 12, verse 32, Jesus says, "And I, if I be lifted up from the earth, will draw all men unto me." John continues in verses 33-34 saying, "This he said, signifying what death He should die. The people answered Him, We have heard out of the law that Christ abideth for ever; and how sayest thou, The Son of man must be lifted up? Who is this Son of man?"

Jesus was talking about being lifted from the earth. What is the meaning of being lifted from the earth? John says He was proclaiming what manner of death he should die, as in lifted up on the cross. Many believers often relate being lifted up, to lifting His name up in praise and worship. This draws many people to Him. It could also mean being lifted up from the earth as from the grave. Because he lives! Because he is alive! People are drawn unto him.

Hebrews 5:8-10 says, "Though he were a Son, yet learned he obedience by the things which He suffered; And being made perfect, He became the author of eternal salvation unto all them that obey Him; Called of God, a high priest after the order of Melchisedec."

Jesus served many and suffered long. His entire ministry was serving people, from washing the disciples' feet to feeding multitudes. He taught them and fed them. These services lifted Him to an authority level, to become the author of eternal salvation. It takes service rendered freely and honestly, to be the authority over something or someone.

Unfortunately today, people view authority positions as positions of ruler-ship and try to operate in them without giving in service. It is a principal. Service is the way to become the authority over something. Author means to begin, or the beginning of something. To initiate something. Authority is to have the power to enforce obedience to something, and for you to be the beginning of that obedience that you are delegated to enforce.

Many people think it means to be in charge over, with a firm hand. With seemingly no thought of the service, you are to provide. This kind of thinking has presented itself in some police officers, and judges in courts of law. Actually, for them, it means they should be the beginning of those to uphold the law such as the biggest servants of the law. They should be the example from which everyone else should learn.

In the church, the senior pastor would be the authority. Reading from 1st Peter 5:3, it says,

"Neither as being lords over God's heritage, but being ensamples to the flock."

God instructs this because he knows people mistake these positions as taking the rule over, as opposed to becoming the biggest servant. The service itself does the lifting. If it is not rendered properly through God, as in willingly and freely from one's heart, with no expectation of gain for oneself, it does not, and will not abound towards one's account or relationship with God.

We see in society today, acknowledgement of police brutality rising. Much of what I believe to be the misunderstanding of the word authority. In this society, it seems to suggest one with authority has a right to rule over another, instead of serving another. If the police would see each person as one they should serve, as opposed to one they can rule over, beat, and even shoot if they deem so, they would probably have less disorder to contend with.

What might be the ratio of people having disorderly conduct following a police beating, or shooting, as opposed to the ratio of people having disorderly conduct following a situation where a disorderly person was treated like a human being with a problem, by the police?

It can very easily appear like those who are delegated to enforce the law, are also they that can cause the law to be offended. And if this could happen, it could also be possible to choose who or what people would do the offending. Some with the delegated authority, and without the necessary and proper understanding of providing service could also very easily use religion, race, or sex, to cause the law to be offended. In turn, causing it to appear like a certain race of people is inferior to certain others, in hopes of it suggesting to the masses that it's just the way they are, or God made them inferior to others. Which is emphatically false according to Acts 17:25-26 which says, "... seeing he (God) gives to all life, breath, and all things; and have made of one blood all nations of men for to dwell on all the face of the earth,"

Satan, the god of this world, has perverted many wonderful things of God to appear as he desires. But it will not last, and will be compensated for due to God's justice through Christ. the author of eternal salvation.

Hebrews 12:2 says, "Looking unto Jesus the author and finisher of our faith; who for the joy that was set before Him endured the cross, despising the shame, and is set down at the right hand of the throne of God."

He is a shelter, a strong tower for those who choose Him. Jesus is God's answer to us for everything needed. And for those who do not choose him, Satan will continue to make a mess of their lives. Calling things as he would have them to be. He uses any and everybody he can to "steal, and to kill, and to destroy." (Ref. John 10:10)

It is unfortunate, however, that some pastors and teachers of the Word have taken on this same misunderstanding of authority from the world; and have lost people from their account to God, by trying to lord and rule over them. In God, there is freedom through Christ Jesus. Here again, the senior pastor is supposed to be the biggest servant in the church. He or she should be the greatest example of serving God. The unconditional service is what will lift him or her, and that happens by the power of God. Many have lifted themselves over the people, and the blessings of God are not upon them. But instead, the bondage of Satan shows on their faces and in their lives.

God is a mighty God! His blessings are rich and powerful! The ability of His word is now! The extensiveness of His power is unlimited! The awesomeness of His greatness is inconceivable!

He has made all things to serve, that they may be empowered by Him.

I believe that everything He made has a serving purpose. From the elements, (air, wind, water, and rain to wash and to cleanse), to the trees and nature (absorption of carbonic acids from the air in photosynthesis) to the animals (protection, food, clothing, etc.) to human beings to give and to help or aid one another. Everything that was made on the earth, was made for mankind to have the use of. (Ref. Gen. 1:26-31)

Many people believe and fight for the rights of animals over the needs of human beings. God never intended for this to be so. He gave dominion over the earth to human beings. Many people have come to love animals, and treat them with the greatest of care over and above the need of a human being. All rights come from God. He is right. (Ref. Deut. 32:4) Notwithstanding, we have a choice and free will that God has given us, and as free-will agents, He will not stop us.

People walk with signs and banners, fighting for their rights. Where did this come from? Who gave people rights? Why do people think that they have rights? Let's ask the question, "who told you that?" The answer is: People believe that they have rights simply because they are "human beings." And that is exactly right. This is because God said it and gave it. God gave dominion over everything to human beings, not animals, or trees, or water, or any of these things some people worship. We are blessed by God to have these things, but they are not our master. If we are to continue in this life with any kind of decency, we must extend ourselves to our fellow human beings.

This happens because we have turned our hearts away from our brothers. We do not see ourselves as our brother's keeper. With the dominion God has given us, we have chosen the animals over ourselves. Some fight with great fervor to save the trees and wildlife and walk by a human being whose heart was created in a way that knows and can feel hurt and pain. One that can understand neglect. What have we done to ourselves? The devaluing of human life is at an all-time high. It is not targeted to any particular group of people as many may think. And it starts in these areas of misguided power, and the allowance of rights to animals and trees and things, before human beings. It is not the will of God, and He is not pleased.

Incorrect or no recognition of God means there is no recognition of anything that He made, with the ability to trust that it is being used for the purpose with which he intended. Some may think that cutting down some trees to make provisions for human beings is not good, but in truth, trees were created and made to serve in more than one capacity. Human beings are the greatest of all creations on the earth (Ref. James 1:18) yet are the only ones that defy their maker.

God has done great and mighty things! His works are unfathomable, immeasurable, and inconceivable! He is GOD! He is our maker! He is our sustainer! He is love! He is the reason we can give, and receive love. What is greater? Who is greater? Who dares to show their ignorance by their defiance of Him?

In many cases, ignorance is a choice. To ignore something or someone is a choice that people make. It's not that the opportunity to learn something has not presented itself. Many have simply chosen to be ignorant of the bible, and the ways of God. Choosing this world's knowledge over what God has said.

Ephesians 3:19 says,

"And to know the love of Christ, which passeth knowledge, that ye might be filled with all the fullness of God."

This is the miraculous works of the Holy Spirit. If you know the love of Christ, you can surpass all learned knowledge, and have all the fullness of God. It is hard for some to believe that things are operating on the earth that are by far more powerful than learned knowledge. Every college, every university, every seminar, every lecture, every theory, every philosophy, every dissertation, every thesis, every book was written, every manuscript, every class, every meeting, and every thought, is subject to a higher power, (Ref. 2 Cor. 10:1-18) and all else, regardless to our immediate response.

The late Rev. Dr. Martin Luther King, Jr. said, "We can all be great because we can all serve." I believe one of his references was no doubt, Matthew 23:11 which says, "But he that is greatest among you shall be your servant."

Because of the obedience of Jesus Christ, for His service well-rendered, God has magnified His Word above his name. (Ref. Psalms 138:2b) Jesus is the Word of God, spoken into manifestation by faith. He was the Word made flesh and dwelled among men. Luke 2:40-52 tells when Jesus was twelve years old, and separated from His parents a few days journey. After three days of searching for Him, they found Him in Jerusalem among doctors holding His own in conversation. They marveled at how much He knew, although He was only a boy. Verse 40 says,

"And the child grew, and waxed strong in spirit, filled with wisdom: and the grace of God was upon Him."

He never went to any universities. I'm not knocking the knowledge one gains from attending schools. It's great, however, I am saying be mindful of how it's applied.

Knowledge is power. The only knowledge some people want to deal with is sense knowledge. The knowledge one gets from his five senses. This knowledge is good as well; everything God made is good, but He didn't stop there. Colossians 1:16-17 says,

"For by Him were all things created, that are in heaven, and that are in earth, visible and invisible, whether they be thrones, or dominions, or principalities, or powers, all things were created by Him: And He is before all things, and by Him, all things consist."

The "visible and invisible" is not limited to sight. It represents all sense knowledge. Many people choose to operate in the visible, and act as though the invisible does not exist, but it does. As a matter of truth, it is by far more powerful than the visible. Anything invisible to the physical eye is visible to the Spirit-man on the inside of us and can be received by a believer in Christ Jesus. All things that exist in the spiritual world where God resides, (or the invisible) are pure, and therefore more powerful than this visible world. If you operate by the Holy Spirit, you know that when you close your eyes to things, are the times you see the best. Meaning, that which you obtain by faith, is greater than that which you obtain by sight.

As Jesus walked the earth, He restored sight to the blind, but He also taught them to have faith, and nothing shall be impossible unto them. (Ref. Matt. 17:20) He fed those who were hungry. He healed them of their diseases. He taught His disciples how to speak to situations and they shall obey. (Ref. Luke 9:1)

There is more than this visible world. He taught them in today's terms, "One ounce of prevention, (which is faith) is better than a pound of cure," (which is visible). He attended to their present physical needs, however, He taught them how to no longer be subjected to them. Galatians 3:13-14 says, "Christ hath redeemed us from the curse of the law, being made a curse for us: for it is written, Cursed is every one that hangeth on a tree: That the blessing of Abraham might come on the Gentiles through Jesus Christ; that we might receive the promise of the Spirit through faith."

This is a great service Jesus has done for all who have and will receive Him. We are now free from the curse of the law, which is poverty, sickness, disease, and death. And any other curses that were a part of the law. This is why Jesus is the Ultimate Authority. His services rendered were greater than all. Philippians 2:6-8 says,

"Who, being in the form of God, thought it not robbery to be equal with God: but made Himself of no reputation, and took upon Him the form of a servant, and was made in the likeness of men: And being found in fashion as a man, He humbled Himself, and became obedient unto death, even the death of the cross."

"Though He were a Son, yet learned He obedience by the things which he suffered; And being made perfect, He became the author of eternal salvation unto all them that obey Him; Called of God a high priest after the order of Melchisedec." (Heb. 5:8-10)

www.ingramcontent.com/pod-product-compliance
Lightning Source LLC
Chambersburg PA
CBHW060333130626
46553CB00003B/993